PRAISE F
DEAD UNC

"A great chapbook drills deep, yielding such vibrant detail that we cannot help but inhabit the world built before us. That's the case of the bracing, strangely beautiful *Dead Uncles*, which proposes a reality (and sur-reality) of a sprawling, intergenerational family whose bonds are inflected by sexual transgression. One dead uncle casts a spell for killing barn mice; another keeps his hold on local office thanks to votes tallied from the 'Cemetery Precinct.' Material that could seem grim in another poet's hands is set a-glimmer here by formal dexterity, bold humor, bright images, and musicality of phrasing."

— Sandra Beasley, author of *Count the Waves*

"Ben Kline's marvelous poems explore various ways men behaved in his world, hovering around the edges of his childhood—tough uncles with their love of sports, chewing tobacco, open flies, and undercurrents of violence. Kline's poetry casts a spell (and even employs spells) to counteract these influences and forge a different path. 'Blessed art thou/ among men who want to in ways/ they've been told they shouldn't.' Blessed are we, the readers of *Dead Uncles*."

— Denise Duhamel, author of *Second Story*

"Ben Kline's *Dead Uncles* is haunted by the history of a place and people. It's a small town and a big family that drinks Dew and spits chew, where some pray to god while some pray on each other. These are poems that raise the dead and murder the living. Kline's language coils and bites like a snake. Read *Dead Uncles* with two hands."

— Heidi Seaborn, author of *An Insomniac's Slumber Party with Marilyn Monroe*

"'A gathering of young cousins is called a pile.' begins *Dead Uncles,* and from there, the reader is pulled into a world where men die young, 'rain brings ruin / and the devil calls / good morning.' Uncles give questionable advice, ghosts run for office, and through it all, 'the copper shimmer of wishes.'"

— Courtney LeBlanc, author of *Beautiful & Full of Monsters*

"In *Dead Uncles,* Kline imagines a new grammar for queer kinship—one that grapples with the tensions between individual and collective memory 'because winners are alleged to write history' even as that history takes on lives of its own. The poems in this collection turn to a sensual archive of pearl lighters, gold Fords, and vellum bibles to search for the avuncular: an intimacy among men that is often only legible in folklore and reverie, 'truth without proof.' Kline reminds us to whom we owe our stories, ones we've learned to tell ourselves because otherwise others will tell them for us or no one else will at all."

— Travis Chi Wing Lau, author of *Paring and The Bone Setter*

"At its tender nucleus, Ben Kline's short and bittersweet *Dead Uncles* is a deeply personal exploration of family. From grandmothers who prophesize to recognizable corpses beneath a mini-mall, Kline's poems place us right there in those rooms; not as a fly on a wall, but as another ghost, ourselves nostalgic for these stories and privileged to inherit them. Imbued with such natural wisdoms passed down through generations, these poems transcend into verses, becoming one family's Testament of which to live by, to celebrate, and most importantly, to heed. Ben Kline is a talent, and I can't wait to see what he does next."

— John Manuel Arias, author of *Where There Was Fire*

"When parents dub their friends as Uncles to their child, it sends a message that family can be earned, attributed. But it works both ways. Kline's *Dead Uncles* highlights these men, some of whom are related, some not, some of which are cautionary tales used to scare the little ones—these men, dead and dying, the ghosts in the barn, the embodiment of lines being crossed—and some perhaps are just outcast and queer like the narrator's burgeoning, and terrifying, sexuality in world where swelter // that feels like heaven and hell. We learn the lessons society, religion, and family expect us to from those who came before us, whether we want to or not. Kline's *Dead Uncles* is immaculate, vital and febrile, it's a keening for an adolescence whose shocks are still being reckoned with, and the best thing he's ever written."

– Mark Ward, author of *Carcass and Circumference*

"In *Dead Uncles*, Ben Kline renders a portrait of a family that 'you must suspend all disbelief' to know: one intergenerational in the matter-of-fact inclusion of its ghosts whose stories are told as if they never ended—as if this book itself were the old recipe or the spell or the secret passed down to keep them alive."

– Clair Dunlap, editor at *Vagabond City Lit*

"Self-labeled as 'Poems / Folklore / Reverie,' Ben Kline's *Dead Uncles* forges a liminal space between our real, lived histories and the fairy tales of the past that we trick ourselves into believing. At the heart of these poems lie uncles who are impish and dangerous in life, who have the audacity to 'wander…complaining about the damp' even in death, and who the speaker must both learn from and survive. Among this cast of imperfect characters, Kline shows us that part of growing up is accepting the flawed and mortal nature of our elders, and eventually ourselves. As uncles give advice, threaten, laugh, live and die, these poems mend the holes they leave behind with sharp wit and sly observations. Kline takes his foot and smears the line between the magical and the grotesque, and it is here that we discover again how to love and how to forgive."

— Taylor Byas, author of *Bloodwarm*

"Ben Kline's *Dead Uncles* is a gorgeously seering exploration of Southern ideals of family, gender, and gentility. Through masterful, magnetic language, Kline magicks even seemingly mundane moments into a lens through which one can see the most imperative truths: how we are harmed, healed, and humbled by the ties that bind us, a force that 'feels like heaven and hell / whether you believe it or not.'"

— Emma Bolden, author of *House Is an Enigma*

"Whether or not you believe in ghosts is none of their business—they've got other things to worry about, and plenty to tell us in *Dead Uncles*. Ben Kline charges his images with menace and lust, scattering them across a landscape that is both dreamlike and disturbingly real, where 'every moment is survival / or not.'"

— Mark Bibbins, author of *13th Balloon*

Ben Kline's
Dead Uncles
Poems / Folklore / Reverie

INDEPENDENTLY PUBLISHED BY
DRIFTWOOD PRESS

Independently published by Driftwood Press
in the United States of America.

Managing Poetry Editor & Interviewer: Jerrod Schwarz
Cover Image: Phil Hale
Cover Design: Sally Franckowiak
Interior Design & Copyeditor: James McNulty
Fonts: Maecenas, Sitka, Garamond, & Merriweather

First published May 2021
ISBN-13: 978-1-949065-11-4

Please visit our website at www.driftwoodpress.net
or email us at editor@driftwoodpress.net.

MISPRINT
(DO NOT RESELL)

For superstition, the truth without proof.

For the uncles and the aunts.

For the pile.

Contents

A Pile

A gathering of young cousins is called a pile. It's not a reunion without aunts and dead uncles. Oak leaves from the same root share a shape, a half-acre, innumerate shades. They play volleyball across a white rope tying two eastern hemlocks. In the cemetery, paper plates become bases. Fingertips and loose fists, static, hair in the eye. A pile, growing.

At a reunion, aunts flit around, scooping limp green beans and macaroni salad onto compartment foam plates. Nothing and no one touches. Uncles roll joints, discuss old girlfriends, dismiss the mill closing before Christmas. Elbows and tight fists. A gathering of dead uncles is called a reverie. It's not a daydream if you must suspend all disbelief.

Dead Uncle, 1979

Hail Marys lobbed at the altar
from the last pew. Only twenty-five.

Light sentence mumbled fast. No beads.
No sweat. I knew Father heard the grin

inside the sleeves of my white tee
rolled like James Dean, cool

red vinyl of the kneeler seeping
into my torn jeans, the sizzle

of votives, naked Jesus. Amen.
He never looked me in the eye

outside the dark booth. I squinted
like Brando in the woods

full of tall, graceful tamaracks,
grateful men. He insisted *You believe*

and behave as if eternity can be that easy
with repetition. Blessed art thou

among men who want to in ways
they've been told they shouldn't.

I practiced languor, forming pearls,
sweat. Men who shouldn't always do

like Montgomery Clift, ruined
by a turn too fast into the hour

of violet sarcomas, dumpsters
overflowing with shriveled uncles,

other men from the park I wandered
in lavender dusk, in swelter

that feels like heaven and hell
whether you believe or not.

Beautitude

You sniffed my hayfield neck,
sifted my midnight curls

but Grandma warned you
I keep no secrets
where rain brings ruin
the devil calls
good morning.

She warned you
when you cornered me,
a yellow rat snake

threading the locust
branches permitting me
passage through thorns.

Hunger has a belly
but covers its ears.
She warned you

would tackle me to the grass,
your pulse against my larynx.

My tongue curled with our sweat,
My incisors tested your elasticity.

Your blood cooled,
a small mirror in the dirt
drowning a lone ant.

Grandma told you what to do
when I asked you
if hunger or the devil
looked back.

Murder

I nailed the panes / salted the hardwood beneath / around the bed / per the flyleaf notes / folded in great grand Nana's vellum bible / If I did not / the murder would / jimmy the locks / sail my breath / What are you / Who is he / I folded my lips in / Why do you / I spoke no names / That rusty afternoon / they found me against a red maple / grunting into my hand / calling for God I could not see / what they slipped in my ribs / Frayed primary / silken covert / toothy blade / another bad idea / Who is he / they had heard before

After months / of winter nights / my jaw ached at waking / I stowed my lost teeth / in clean socks / I pulverized them / for the floor / I wrote no notes / burned my clipped nails / collected curls from the sink / pillows / underwear / If I did not / they would / Coal beaks / gnawing cuticle / oil / DNA / loose in the wind / above the west field / blue timothy swaying / too close to the creek / It swelled every May / overt / but forgetful

When they came / two at each window / heads twisting to see / I covered my face / I bit my tongue / What are you / more rust / Who is he / I pulled the hammer / from under two sheets / my quilt / Why do I / its weight on my chest / lingering / like him / No name / Why am I / waiting for them / to caw / to scratch / Most violence / I have heard before / flutters unnamed

P i p e r

Cheddar cubes, powdered
zinc phosphide, a splash

of antifreeze fill
the red wheelbarrow

as Dad instructed.
Arabicas in palm

protect my nose
atop a rear tractor tire

under the tin shed
he built in '85. The tire

wobbles as rubber does.
The mice will climb

the tray in time. I brought
a couple frozen cans of Dew.

I shoo the terriers, the calico
who winks, my little siblings.

I tighten my cap.
Two, three, five, eight

and more find the cheese.
It's not my favorite.

The wind won't keep
this odor, only carry it.

Eleven, twenty. Mom warned
about ghosts in the barn,

brown owls, corn snakes
who act like uncles, dodging

the barrow because temptation
is a lie, a new moon,

thunder the fifty-one
don't hear as they seize

and pop. Cataracts cloak
their gaze. Two tumble out,

dust blooms. I ferry them
to the mud hole I dug

under the garden oak, tipping
the barrow, ooze and fur,

little yellow headstones.
Dad grins, eyes wide, white.

You did good, he says.
Everything's great again.

Will / Inherit

Suddenly / late summer / shirtless in the loft / he watches me /
surmount the top rung / Soft timothy exhaling June / The twine
breaks / spreading blue / purple florets on which we lie / about men
/ the Virgin / glistening skin / senators and welfare / other things we
cannot carry / like pistols / plastic bags / creek mud when it floods /
uncovering July's empty cans / our fathers' distal bits / shredded
mineral deeds / gold watches and fillings / silver rings my nephews
will inherit / as we leave / behind nothing

Uncle Lucky

told me to *wear the same white knee highs*
Sunday service through Friday morning,
even if Mom upends drawers, hamper
and mattress. Rub sliced onions
on my armpits. *Helps the hair grow too.*
Eat banana pudding with grape wine
from Granny's cellar. Cross my fingers
when I sneak it to my room. Drink cider
vinegar diluted with warm Mellow Yellow
before Thursday scrimmage, no matter
the humidity or heat in my cleats.
That combustion is science no one
owns, magic older than Lucky's mama
Agnes, named for a third cousin on her nana's
married side. *Keep your dick out*
of a teammate's ear and in my hand.
Be nice to my sisters, my cousins,
the reverend, the other uncles
at the game in their muddy boots,
black hard hats, unbuttoned
holsters, standing to cheer
points I score. Spit chew next
to the opposing linemen's shoes.
Speak in tongues to signal plays.
Distract the deputies with a two-point
conversion, dancing the end zone
Hallelujah, arms over my head,
Lucky on his way out, handing
a wad of Jacksons
to the visiting coach.

Giving Up the Dew

Sneak through straight rain
into dusk's silver linger.
Find two wigglers surfaced,
pink, pale as raw chicken.
Pick them from grass,

never concrete. Give them
the names of your best former lovers.
Chop them into even fourths.
Drop each gooey eighth
into a red plastic cup.

Add two pinches of sodium
chloride and bicarbonate,
a churned mouthful of spit,
one flake of willow bark
to all eight.

Cross the pasture
as they stew. Collect
four half cups of ditch water.
Avoid leaves, drowned squirrels,
dry raven feathers atop the stream.

On your way back, yank
a tuft of bloomed fescue.
Shred it with your lower
left incisor, the one
you chipped in our Christmas fight.

Once home repeat
those lovers' names
three times as you drool
your weed cud into the second
and fifth cups. Wash your hands.

Chug the first half cup
from the ditch. Quickly,
holding your breath.
Sip the second, the third,
a fourth if you can.

Your belly might swell.
Your flank might rumble.

God or Satan might
come through
with fire. Rest

until you cool, ghosts climbing
out your lungs, whispering
midmorning, Father, too
close, myrrh, fist,
thunder.

Cemetery Precinct

Mom calls the graveyard beside my school a cemetery precinct. Not because she works the polling station in the gymnasium every November, completing ballots for our uncles in the east line of faded tombstones. Or because winners are alleged to write history. *For the family,* she insists, stuffing sheets from her purse into the machine.

The graves are too close for our tall people, bejeweled by dental fillings, shallow to sinkholes, hiding places for sophomores anxious to be voted Most Likeable or Best Shade. Their dead are names we inherit, sometimes edit in the 977.1 section at the library. Mom says we have to keep Uncle Linus in office. *Think it through.*

I imagine the cemetery under a strip mall, school kids at a new froyo shop, kissing with icy lips to select a class treasurer. The graves accessible in the sub-basement. Uncle Linus propped in the corner, slack white mandible holding a "Vote FIELD for Progress" sign. Ghosts wander the tunnel, around the walk-in freezer, complaining about the damp.

Polygraph

A hot knife only hurts if you're lying, Uncle Meade mumbled
around his chew, the flame from his pearl lighter

licking its blade red. Icicles plinked from the gutters. My hand
remained closed in my coat pocket,

blue smolder curling from the bullet hole into the hayloft.
And lying only causes more hurt

than it's worth. He tilted, watched the plasma bend around the steel.
I wondered if Einstein had it wrong,

had confused gravity and light with truth and beauty. Saliva flowed
through my missing teeth. My tongue

drowned. *So you should just tell me now.* I knew his blade
would cool quickly in the pink January sunset,

that I could lose him in the oakwood shadows. He grinned.
I waited.

W a k e

Wilfred passed. Overnight an ice storm stripped the pines, embalmed a thousand fallow acres.

Dad drove the gold Ford. Mom, baby T and Grandma crammed in the cab, Sis and me in the back peeking from under a tarp. Our valley prismatic, diamond guts. Orange and yellow-white beams ricocheted between blade tips gleaming

like hungry raccoons, watching ghosts, aliens of nitrous composition waiting

to take me away. *Everyone's in the den.* Technicians in beige coveralls said *Slowly now, careful,* his body under bone sheets floating on the gurney.

Reverend Jenkins whispered hellos, *He's gone home,* shook hands, *How's the mine,* other benedictions. *Let us pray.* Everyone huddled,

rosaries in hand, an absence of angles off which to pivot away.

Cousin Dan poured his father's last two bottles of whiskey into thirty-one clear plastic cups, the carpet, the slinking calico. His chance to let everyone know.

To Wilfred. Dad nodded. Liquid brass filled my throat.

Our Father who art, second sip stunned my tongue, trapped the next line in my lungs, close to my left atrium, *give us this day,* my kingdom alveoli, power and glory and faith away.

The ice remained for two days of blue skies, *forever and ever*, the same northward sun, no one whispering, *Quickly, it's your chance.*

Be Prepared

Scaling an oak on the government land uncle Ray claimed
was stolen from great Grandpa, a robin's G-sharp strikes
my incus. My fingers shred bark. A hiss of cavils
splits my tongue. Tremors straighten my toes
and seal my throat. Her A-sharp knells
behind my eyes, a pterodactyl whisper
about forged deeds, Ray's breath,
the Chicxulub shattering the mesosphere,
everything afire. I ignore the black plumes,
holding my breath, hanging
by my knees.

In the bluegrass an earthworm thrashes
toward God. The robin dives,
beak wide, ready to show me
every moment is survival
or not. The worm's guts
spill faded blades,
sunny mud, other
glossy bits.

My bare legs
rush the fescue.
The worm had
no idea.

Home, I splash cold water on my face
and check the packed bag
under the bed.

Men Who Lay Hands

Between sips of neat whiskey
in the porch swing overlooking
the soybeans sprouting too close
to the creek, Aunt Martha whispered:

> Go find ten ladybugs (specifically, I learned later,
> *harmonia axyridis.*)

> Pluck their sheer underwings. Grind those in a black
> bowl, (ceramic if you got it.)

> Drip in two tablespoons of water skimmed from the
> deep end of the pond up top the near hill (where algae
> shimmers blue when sunrise scrubs the world.)

> Set the mixture outside the oak shade for the hottest
> hour of that day before you add oil, honey. Whip it
> creamy as swished spit.

> Place the bowl by his salad at dinner. Let him pour.

> He'll sniff it and taste it with his pointer and use it all.
> He'll call it sweet as that smack between your cheese fat
> thighs. He'll lap the bowl, licking the rim and his fin
> gers, smiling so wide you'll know it's working. Slowly
> though.

Seven days to a week later, he'll pass in his sleep.
Cardiac arrest. Peaceful as a puppy after an hour
paddling the creek. No doctor will guess, and it depends
on him if he goes to Jesus or the Devil, because no matter
a man's actions,

you can never know his heart.

I nodded, smiled because my mom
taught me to keep that secret, too,
and I asked, *Should I get my honey
from the barn hive?*

No, Martha said, her empty tumbler
wrapped in crooked red acrylics,
*use store bought. Keep that good stuff
for yourself.*

Euchre

Uncle Ricky revealed the savvy of an open fly
at the Labor Day cookout, spreading his legs, his shaved balls

smacking the bench, Mom and cousin Janice talking casserole
until two gasps and *Well now,* a rare agreement.

Freeballing *exponents* the success of a bluff, aunt Maddie insisted.
She refilled my cup with *strong water* from Ricky's two-liter of Diet Sprite.

She saw his dick and shrugged. I could relate
to her always calling on spades, how she said *savior fairy,* slurping

through her diastema, showing too many teeth, counting the deal
in the chrome of his Zippo. He blinked too

fast through his weak cut, perfunctory shuffles, cigar fumes, five
stepsons with three-syllable names he didn't know. He said *shit far* a lot.

How far? They laughed. I kept my drink, three cigarettes, an extra Jack
of Spades between my thighs to thwart a farmer's hand.

My Uncle-in-Law's Third Stepchild

wears spaghetti strap tank tops, clear
packing tape lifting their narrow chest.

They scrape rusty backyard handlebars
to smoke their eyelids, the copper

shimmer of wishes left face down
in the mall fountain where they film

their micro video clips, splashing blue
from the basin, slicking their pink hair,

curling their seventeen black lace bracelets,
a strip for every year their father complains,

Why do you have your sister's lips?
His nose scrunches when I suggest

maybe their sister has their lips.

Dead at 46

If I die as predicted
by my great grandmother's ghost—

a car crash three minutes
after I turn forty-six—

fold my remains
into a hand sewn book

about a city girl's eldest child
crossing several state lines,

Dad's purple Chevy tearing up
and the map, the phone book

scanned for motels, overlooks,
safe places for Mom to puke.

If I die that Wednesday afternoon—
another distant uncle gone—

I hope it doesn't hurt,
hope I hover embryonic,

a meteor ghost burning up
no closer to heaven

than when Mom prayed
for a boy without bend.

She was too Catholic
to choose a red edit.

If I die as the other driver
speeds away–

will I hear their engine,
the birds, my slowing pulse?

Don't let the paramedics
lower my lids.

I want the light to fill
my pupils revealing

the other side, the spiral
galaxy of the ether.

But if I die another way
on another date–Nana was known

to bourbon her black tea–
I hope it's by choice

after medicine fails,
under stiff sheets,

bad fluorescents, sharing
a room at the nursing home

with Mom, half joking about who
will pull the plug on whom.

Part Time Jobs in Appalachia

I do-si-doed round another Saturday afternoon at the ass end of Goose Creek. Down bank the Orlando Mule with a Hitler tattoo and a grip I didn't resist made me listen to "Billie Jean" for the fiftieth time. I spun on my heel like I meant it from my hips like a tease, the river marooning flotsam on the boat ramp behind us. I hollered *Eeee heee!* at an octave too high to echo across the river where real vice evaded arrest with intent to distribute at the park & ride and truckers idled their rigs for lizards coming through the lot in freight shadows. Muncie Semi Guy grabbed my thigh, growled *You're getting a little too big,* picking up the scent of the new thicket below the ripped waist of my Wranglers. I took a pouty drag off his joint, dropped to my knees in his sleeper next to his blue and white cooler of Coors Light and Snickers, holding my breath when near his damp basement pits. He always wore ribbed grey tanks. He counted the black mollies I arranged on a white towel: two, five, ten until he yanked me by my curls, flinging three crisp twenties and a Lincoln tip at me faster than any silver haired teller craving a smoke on her break. Two more sales and I returned to the ramp with my 150% of trickle up and Hawaiian Tropic, stripping to tight white Hanes and my Reds cap over my face, listening to the barge waves slap the limestone until Deputy Jenkins idled up asking *How much did you make?*

Enough for your cut and mine, uncle.

I undo the past by breathing underwater,

my city uncle's saltwater pool
a dram of sea

from which we crawled
without limbs
to light.

I undulate my arms and dream the future
in this familiar blue-

green again, the depth
compressing the spectrum and my thoughts

back together, to see
what glowed

inside the sun, moon or stars
before we named them.

Bubbles gurgle from my nose.

My uncle repeats my name
in the light,

a whale's sigh
I mimic with one breath, two

filling me with origin forgotten
inside my sequence,
my helix pink

the color of burn after a day afloat.

I have not found the future
by my undoing. The water

holds me close, tight
as my father crying

in the dark, my chest emptied
of space, explanation

or chance.

If it's bitter at the start

why pick up the knife?
Dull, sharp or rusted,
I kept the serrated side
turned away. I kept
a loose grip, let the cousins
at the cookout believe
what they were seeing.
Mom told the uncles
I practiced *redneck tricks,*
perched on the fence
in my jorts, no shirt, gold
cross dangling, slipping
the steel blade between
my knuckles, the bevel
tumbling purlicue to pinky.
She used to gauze my hands
when I messed up the flip,
my eyes when my gaze lingered
on men in the feed store
parking lot. Dad said,
His alligator eyes're too big
for his hummingbird ass.
But I never felt more than
the exaggeration my lips
and bare fingers made
in the air, risking certain
defeat by getting what

I thought I wanted.
When I caught the tang
in my teeth, they lifted
their hats. Most clapped.
Mom returned her gauze
to her purse. *Blood,* Dad said,
is not always a sign of glory,
especially if you're losing it.
Up close, under shreds
of gauze, fine pink lines
from years of practice,
waving too soon, forming
the names of those men
who looked back, hoping
it's sweeter in the end.

Corpse Reviver

Seeing isn't always knowing

past a rainy Monday night's fourth corpse reviver #2, circling back
to dead uncles I resemble when I slick my dark curls

like I'm *too cool for school*, as Uncle Craig used to
drag his 00's until Marlboros ate his throat in that warm December.

The future isn't always

messy, Big Rich's midday widow maker
accelerating his Cadillac through a Dallas intersection,

killing him, a pigeon, three strangers that April Tuesday. I don't know
anything about those strangers.
I don't know their names
or see them falling

in love with a nurse after the second Battle of the Hook, their blood
splattering the windshield.
They remain mysterious

like Uncle Joe that swampy August Friday the deputies found him
prostrate in a raft on Crystal Lake,

missing his pants, his left pinky, a grand of his boss's snow.

I only saw his stiff limbs and closed fists,
uncle Rick counting pills, placing them
in neat rows. No amount of knowing

changes the outcome: dead uncles
blue in the face, red
leaving their lips.

There are many aspects of *Dead Uncles* that I'm excited to explore, but I think starting with the collection's subheading is a wonderful jumping off point. "Poems / Folklore / Reverie" creates a dynamic trichotomy of what readers can expect to find in these pages. What were your reasons for framing *Dead Uncles* this way? How does poetry differ from folklore and reverie?

Many of the poems gleaned inspiration from the folklore, old wives' tales, family myths, and superstitions of my Appalachian youth. In exploring those phenomena, the poems developed the drowsy quality of reverie and daydreams. "Men Who Lay Hands" and "Beatitude" embody this most obviously, but the others all draw upon that framework.

Also, the "Poems/Folklore/Reverie" frame directs readers into the fantastic nature of the work. These poems have no intention to represent reality. I wanted them to walk right up to the line where they could become ghoulish or phantasmagoric, but do not. They stop at points where you might have to suspend your disbelief, yet waver like highway heat, leaving you unsure of what you see and hear.

I cannot speak on whether poetry differs from folklore or reverie beyond format and intent. All three are often about sharing or imbuing a feeling, an experience the author wishes to share.

As the title suggests, family is at the crux of this collection. What are the hardest and easiest parts of writing about extended family members? Did you always intend to collect these poems, or did the focus reveal itself afterward?

I would not claim that the work in *Dead Uncles* is specifically about my family.

More pointedly, I wanted to excavate, question, and develop a better understanding of adjacent familial relationships. What is the difference between how we are with our uncles than with our fathers? That sort of thing. I have long been fascinated by how these relationships, in my experience, can often have more nuance than what we experience with immediate family. They have fewer rules or expectations, more space for variety in how we interact. In exploring that, these poems pluck details and moods from my own life, from my very large and colorful extended family. That was the easiest part: the lake of ideas. The hardest part was maintaining my focus on the relationships and nuances while not making the poems about actual people who might read them and become upset.

I wrote an entire suite of poems about uncles, aunts, grandparents, cousins, in-laws, etc. Then, the poems in this collection coalesced to focus on uncles, dead ones specifically, in the winter before the pandemic. (I still have dozens of poems about aunts, grandparents, cousins, and more in various other projects and draft files.)

The rural settings in many of these poems feel both serene and quasi-dangerous. As someone who grew up on a small farm, I immediately gravitated toward these beautiful, haunting descriptions of an idyllic but untrustworthy landscape. Where does place and geography fit int your own writing practice? Which aspects of these locations did you want to emphasize? Which aspects did you want to exclude?

I grew up on a large cattle farm in the west Appalachian foothills in the late 1970s and 1980s. A working farm with big equipment and feedlots, acres and acres of crops, pasture and dense forest, isolated from most of the world. (Even now, no cell reception.) It was a serene, fully dangerous and specific place to grow up. Utilizing that in my work, portraying the scale, the visual and spiritual contrasts, all the peculiarities, feels instinctual. I cannot imagine writing a poem without it having a sense of place and space.

For *Dead Uncles*, my place and space emphasis focused on the micro—the locust tree, the bedroom, the ditch, the wake, the rest area, the sulfur lake of an abandoned strip mine. (Note how activities become a space with discernable geography, as in "Euchre" and "I undo the past by breathing underwater.") I wanted these small aspects to have cinematic scope when possible. With proper lighting and sound design, room for an entire poem.

I excluded most of the danger, the violence. Well, except for the ladybugs.

Many of the poems in *Dead Uncles* effortlessly intersect with insights into faith and identity. One of my favorite sections reads "red vinyl of the kneeler seeping / into my torn jeans, the sizzle / of votives, naked Jesus." Are these topics consistent themes throughout all of your poetics, or are they specific to *Dead Uncles*?

I own the interpolation of faith and identity appearing in some manner in all my work. Consider that my earliest inspirations were Prince, Madonna, Anne Sexton, Larry Kramer, Anne Rice, Robert Mapplethorpe, Thom Gunn, and Joe Bolton. I believe those themes appear with different intentions and varied forms in my other work, maybe lacking the specific relationship they share throughout *Dead Uncles*.

As an editor, I am often asked to explain the specifics of a prose poems. Outside of pointing students in the direction of strong examples, this form can often feel illusory and undefined. *Dead Uncles* is home to wonderful prose poems throughout, and I want to ask how you approach this mystifying form? What are advantages and disadvantages of a prose poem? What does your process look like when drafting one?

I began my writing life as a fiction writer in high school, through college, for a decade thereafter. I loved novellas and flash fiction most. I wanted to write short fiction collections, win an O. Henry or two, give readings in New York and San Francisco. But when prompted by teachers/professors for poetry, I saw prose poems as my form of choice. (Lineation, as a concept, still feels like sorcery to me.) For me, prose poems happen when you mix old-fashioned fireside storytelling with poetry's purposeful invocations of imagery and music. They should not feel written; they should feel planned, staged, and performed. I approach them as such.

I find two main advantages to prose poetry: accessibility and volume. By accessibility, I find that more non-poets can enter prose poems and "get them." When I share work with friends who are not poets, they gravitate toward the prose poems. I believe that comes from a prose poem seeming both familiar in its form and less intimidating than more traditionally organized poetry. And by volume, I mean that you can include much more information in a prose poem than, say, a sparse, precise sonnet in couplets, and you can deploy poetic devices in more robust ways.

The big disadvantage to a prose poem is the risk of your poetic melody being swallowed in a block of text or sentences.

One of my favorite ways to dig into a work is to study its word frequency. While there is not always a relationship between frequency and theme, I was interested to find that "dead" was one of the more common words in the collection. What is the significance of this word to you and your writing? Are there any words that stand out as more emblematic in your mind?

"Dead" is significant in this collection because, from the title to the final poem, "Corpse Reviver," I wanted the reader to interpret all the work as being in memoriam. The metaphoric dead uncles are memories, folklore, reverie. They haunt, inspire, and inform.

I suppose I think a lot about the dead. I was an older grandchild in my large family, meaning I knew and had relationships with many of the elders my youngest siblings and cousins never knew. I think I had attended a dozen funerals before I could drive. And I was a teen during the worst of the AIDS crisis. Too many dead uncles then. So *dead* and the dead will always be a part of my work.

As for other words, you made me look: "uncle" and "hand" appear the most in *Dead Uncles*. (I am that writer who uses Control + F to make sure I do not overutilize certain verbs, adjectives, or phrases.) I know I employ "used to" a lot in drafts. Because so much of my work ponders how it was, is, and might be. That pivot from "used to."

How long had you been working on this collection? What did your first draft of the chapbook look live versus the final manuscript?

Dead Uncles began on July 4, 2018 according to my "hillbilly spell poetry drafts" in Google Drive. That was the day I wrote "Men Who Lay Hands" and another poem (a poem I ended up cutting, even though it was published by the journal *Toe Good*, because I detest the ending and have yet to craft an improvement.) I called them spell poems because of the inspirations mentioned earlier. They proved popular at readings. I was writing one or two new ones a week; many ended up in *Twang*, my full length manuscript. Many more wait for future projects.

The first draft of *Dead Uncles* (titled *Back Holler Magic*) was longer and more sexual, more brutal even. It felt more in time, where this "final" version floats in and out of time. This final sequencing came together at the beginning of the COVID-19 pandemic, when my brain could not conjure the magic anymore, and I found my poems revisiting the AIDS crisis years again.

Often times, you will hear authors make the contentious statement that they are moving on to new concerns in their writing. Are there any concerns in *Dead Uncles* that you feel finished with or no longer care to write about? Inversely, what moments from this chapbook do you want to keep investigating?

I am not finished with any of the concerns in this book. I have this idea for a novella inspired by "Cemetery Precinct." I have written about three poems in direct relation or response to "A Pile." (Something I picked up from Prince, whose songs, especially the old bootlegs, were often in dialogue with one another.) I intend to put none of this to rest. I will continue to ask questions, explore, excavate. My take on and reaction to the dead uncle changes as I age. How I interact with the hillbilly magic shifts. What was once curse become cure.

Also, I tend to work on three or four projects simultaneously. I was finishing my astrophysics/time travel chapbook *Sagittarius A** while working on *Dead Uncles*. I might move on to different concerns, but I tend to return, revisit, revise. I blame my Gemini nature.

More to that above point, what is next for Ben Kline? Simply, what are you working on right now, and how might it differ from the concerns of *Dead*

Uncles?

Next for me is more poetry and (fingers crossed) finally putting together a short fiction collection.

I continue to submit and shop my full-length manuscript, *Twang*. I have two chapbooks in progress: one about our health care system, our wellness, chronic pain, and the evils of insurance. The other plays on non-standard forms in poetry. I have those many dead uncle/hillbilly spell drafts to revisit and do something with at some point. Maybe a sequel: Aunt Hill? Unnamed Nephews? Grand Ghosts?

What advice do you have for other poets? What are strategies, mantras, or bits of guidance that have helped in your practice as a poet?

My advice is always to be disciplined, have purpose, and socialize.

By *discipline*, I mean be consistent and practice your craft. Daily, weekly, whatever. Just have a schedule to make it feel like a part of what you do. Practice. Do what you do well but try new things too.

By *have purpose*, know why you want to write. Think about what you want to say. Even if you may not know what you want to say until you have arrived at it. Even if your answer is *For the glory and the power* or *To change humanity*. Just have purpose. Writing just to write is…well, work. Having purpose elevates your work to art.

By *socialize*, find your fellow poets. Share work. Read theirs. Exchange notes. Talk craft. And, go to readings—virtual and in person.

Where can readers find more of your work?

I would recommend my website's Publications, Media & Events page. It contains links to many of my individual poems and publications, as well as readings, speaking engagements, other projects, and much more (benklineonline.wordpress.com).

> **The above interview with Ben Kline was conducted via email by Jerrod Schwarz.**

ACKNOWLEDGEMENTS

Thank you to the following publications in which some of these poems (or earlier versions of them) appeared:

"A Pile" *Queen Mob's Teahouse, 2020*
"Dead Uncle, 1979" *A&U Magazine,* 2020
"Murder" *Driftwood Press,* 2021
"Will/Inherit" *Vagabond City Lit,* 2019
"Giving Up the Dew" *Alien Literary Magazine,* 2020
"Men Who Lay Hands" *Riggwelter,* 2019
"Cemetery Precinct" *perhappened mag,* 2020

Thank you to the team at *Driftwood Press* for their support and time, their care for this collection.

Special thanks to Aaron Libby, Todd Dillard, Holly Prochaska, Melissa Norris, Crystal Ignatowski, John Byrne, Tyler French, Cyndie Randall and many more for their input and support of this project.

Ben Kline lives in Cincinnati, Ohio. He is the author of *Sagittarius A** and *Going Fast in Loose Directions*. His poetry and prose have appeared in *DIAGRAM, Hobart, The Cortland Review, A&U Magazine* and elsewhere.

CPSIA information can be obtained
at www.ICGtesting.com
Printed in the USA
LVHW102049220621
690896LV00003B/31

9 781949 065114